The Science of
RENEWABLE
ENERGY

THE SCIENCE OF
HYDROGEN ENERGY
by Yvette LaPierre

ReferencePoint
Press®

San Diego, CA

© 2018 ReferencePoint Press, Inc.
Printed in the United States

For more information, contact:
ReferencePoint Press, Inc.
PO Box 27779
San Diego, CA 92198
www.ReferencePointPress.com

Library of Congress Cataloging-in-Publication Data

Names: LaPierre, Yvette, 1963- author.
Title: The science of hydrogen energy / by Yvette LaPierre.
Description: San Diego, CA : ReferencePoint Press, Inc., [2018] | Series: The
  science of renewable energy | Includes bibliographical references and
  index.
Identifiers: LCCN 2017042005 | ISBN 9781682823057 (hardcover : alk. paper) |
  ISBN 9781682823064 (pdf)
Subjects: LCSH: Hydrogen as fuel--Juvenile literature.
Classification: LCC TP359.H8 L37 2018 | DDC 665.8/1--dc23
LC record available at https://lccn.loc.gov/2017042005

IMPORTANT EVENTS IN THE DEVELOPMENT OF
HYDROGEN ENERGY

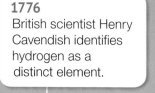

1950s
NASA begins using liquid hydrogen as a rocket fuel.

1998
Iceland unveils its plan to become the first hydrogen-based economy.

1776
British scientist Henry Cavendish identifies hydrogen as a distinct element.

1959
Fuel cell transportation begins with the building of the first practical fuel cell and the demonstration of the first fuel cell vehicle, a tractor.

1770	1800	1950	1960	1970

1800
Scientists William Nicholson and Sir Anthony Carlisle discover the process of electrolysis.

1970s
Electrochemist John Bockris coins the phrase *hydrogen economy*.

1800s
Sir William Grove, an English scientist, invents the gas battery, which is later renamed the fuel cell.

1994
Daimler-Benz demonstrates the first fuel cell car, a minivan.

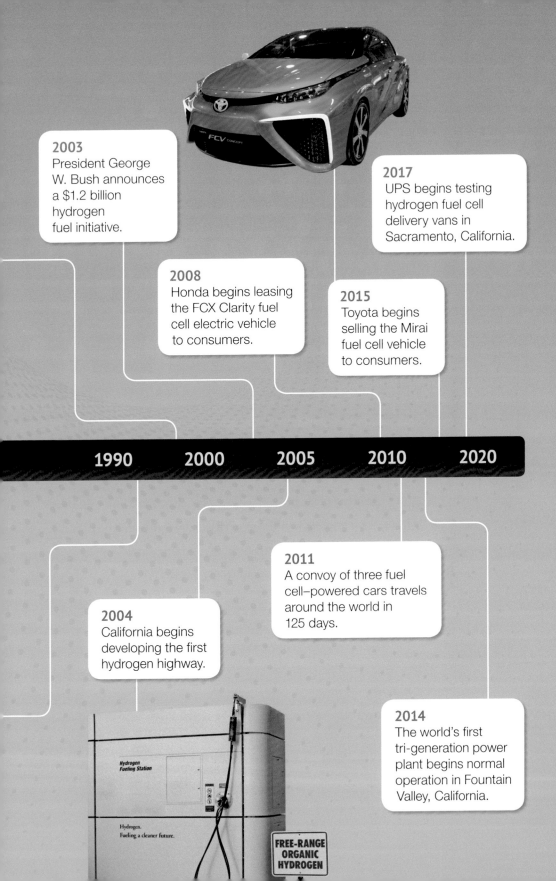

2003
President George W. Bush announces a $1.2 billion hydrogen fuel initiative.

2017
UPS begins testing hydrogen fuel cell delivery vans in Sacramento, California.

2008
Honda begins leasing the FCX Clarity fuel cell electric vehicle to consumers.

2015
Toyota begins selling the Mirai fuel cell vehicle to consumers.

1990 2000 2005 2010 2020

2011
A convoy of three fuel cell–powered cars travels around the world in 125 days.

2004
California begins developing the first hydrogen highway.

2014
The world's first tri-generation power plant begins normal operation in Fountain Valley, California.

Hydrogen Fueling Station

Hydrogen. Fueling a cleaner future.

FREE-RANGE ORGANIC HYDROGEN

NATURE'S FUEL

FROM THEORY TO APPLICATION

Hydrogen is the most abundant element in the universe. Inside stars, it powers the process that generates heat and light. On Earth, hydrogen is only naturally found in compound form with other elements. Water, for example, is made up of molecules containing two hydrogen atoms and one oxygen atom. When hydrogen is separated out of a compound, the pure hydrogen gas can be stored. Combining hydrogen with oxygen causes a chemical reaction that creates water and releases energy. This energy can be converted into electricity. There are two ways to do this. Hydrogen gas can be used in a combustion engine similar to the ones in gasoline-powered cars. Hydrogen gas can also be combined with oxygen in a fuel cell. This is the more efficient option. In a fuel cell, the reaction is carefully controlled. It produces electricity with only water vapor and heat as by-products.

Wherever people live, there's waste. Society generally thinks of waste as something that must be disposed of. But waste contains significant amounts of energy. Today, people are turning to new ways of harvesting this energy. A power plant in Fountain Valley, California, a suburb of Los Angeles, turns sewage waste into electricity. The Fountain Valley energy station uses biogas produced by the Orange County Sanitation District's municipal wastewater treatment plant. This biogas, which consists largely of methane, is the result of organic waste **fermenting**. The Fountain Valley power plant uses a fuel cell to turn the biogas into three products: heat, electricity, and hydrogen gas. This capability makes the plant the world's first tri-generation system. Scott Samuelsen, director of the research center behind the power plant, said, "This is a paradigm shift. This is the epitome of sustainability, where we're taking an endless stream of human waste and transforming it to transportation fuel."[1]

WORDS IN CONTEXT

fermenting
Undergoing a chemical breakdown by bacteria, yeasts, or other microorganisms.

The electricity generated by the fuel cell power station powers the wastewater treatment plant. The hydrogen gas is captured, compressed for easy transportation, and sent to an on-site public filling station for fuel cell vehicles (FCVs). The power plant produces approximately 220 pounds (100 kg) of hydrogen gas per day. That's enough to fuel up to fifty FCVs. In 2014, when the plant opened, the price of hydrogen in California was about ten dollars per kilogram, roughly equal to the price of gasoline on a per-mile basis.

This photo shows the innovative, high-tech Fountain Valley facility. The key benefits of its tri-generation system are low emissions and high efficiency.

The Fountain Valley energy station has a few important benefits. First, the energy is produced from a renewable resource: biogas. Second, the energy is produced on-site and entirely from local resources. That means that neither the resources going into nor the resources coming out of the plant require long-distance transportation. Transporting these resources would add expense to the process and do additional harm to the environment.

The Fountain Valley energy station was supported in part by a $2.2 million grant from the US Department of Energy (DOE) and is operated by a company called FuelCell Energy. Jack Brouwer of the University of California, Irvine, who worked with FuelCell Energy on the plant for more than a decade, was excited to see the project finally finished in 2014. "Not everyone starts to work on an idea in 2001 and then sees it go all the way to a reality—to actually powering a wastewater treatment plant and putting zero emission fuel into fuel-cell vehicles that are zero emissions themselves," he said. "Come on, this is pretty awesome."[2]

Hydrogen Energy Today

Projects such as Fountain Valley demonstrate that hydrogen energy can be produced and delivered locally, efficiently, and cleanly. Successful tri-generation power plants may be the bridge to creating the infrastructure needed to make hydrogen a viable energy source for the future.

Currently in the United States, approximately 11 million short tons (10 million metric tons) of hydrogen are produced every year. Almost all of it is for industrial use. Industries use it to refine petroleum, process foods, power welding tools, and produce fertilizer, ammonia, and other products. Another use for hydrogen is as a fuel for space exploration. The National Aeronautics and Space Administration (NASA) has used hydrogen to fuel its rockets since the 1950s. Super-cooled liquid hydrogen combined with liquid oxygen has been used to launch space shuttles and other vehicles. NASA notes that "liquid hydrogen yields the highest . . . efficiency in relation to the amount of propellant consumed, of any known rocket propellant."[3]

Some prototype FCVs look vastly different from everyday cars. Others are nearly indistinguishable from most cars on the road.

These applications have made hydrogen a valuable element, but many people see another potential use for it: clean energy. Hydrogen fuel cells have the potential to supply power for a wide variety of things, from small devices such as cell phones and laptops to vehicles and even whole buildings. Hydrogen power is already in use at some data centers, warehouses, farms, and breweries.

Is a Hydrogen Economy Feasible?

Scientist John Bockris coined the phrase "hydrogen economy" in the 1970s.[4] Since then, many scientists and researchers have dreamed of an economy based on this abundant and clean source of energy. Despite its great potential, though, the hydrogen economy has been slow to grow. Unlike other energy resources, pure hydrogen doesn't occur naturally on Earth. Instead, it has to be made, and that process can be expensive in terms of both environmental impact and money. One scientist notes, "It's going to be a terrible environmental solution if we emit water out of the tailpipe, but throughout the whole process emit natural gas."[5] In addition, a vast infrastructure to produce, store, and deliver hydrogen will need to be built if the gas is to be used on a large scale.

These challenges are daunting. They have led to the DOE cutting back on its hydrogen research in recent years. Still, companies and universities are making progress with technologies to make hydrogen energy less expensive and more efficient. Several automobile companies are bringing commercial FCVs to the market. According to researchers at the University of California, Davis, the number of FCVs on the road in California could reach 250,000 around the year 2025. New technologies and innovations are getting us closer and closer to a hydrogen economy.

HOW DOES HYDROGEN
ENERGY WORK?

Hydrogen is the simplest element in the universe. Its symbol on the periodic table is H. A typical hydrogen atom contains one proton and one electron. Protons have a positive charge, and electrons have a negative charge. These charges normally balance each other out. But sometimes an atom of hydrogen loses its electron. Because it has lost a negative charge, the atom's overall charge becomes positive. An atom that has more or less electrons than its default number is called an ion. A hydrogen atom that has lost an electron is known as a hydrogen ion. It is written as H^+.

Besides being the simplest element, hydrogen is also the most abundant. Stars consist primarily of hydrogen, and hydrogen is found in many chemical compounds on Earth. Astrophysicist Neil deGrasse Tyson explains, "Out of the 94 naturally occurring elements, hydrogen lays claim to more than two-thirds of all the atoms in the human body, and more than ninety percent of all atoms in the cosmos, right on down to the solar system."[6]

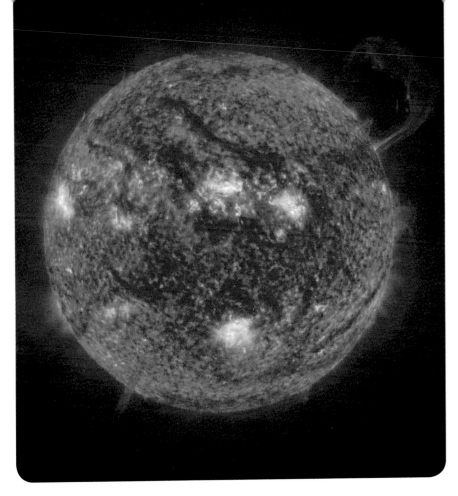

The Sun is approximately 75 percent hydrogen. This hydrogen provides the fuel that has kept the Sun shining for billions of years.

Hydrogen has no smell, color, or taste. As a result, it cannot be perceived by human senses. Hydrogen is the lightest element. It is so light that any hydrogen released on Earth rises through the atmosphere and escapes Earth's gravity. At normal temperature and pressure conditions on Earth, hydrogen is a gas. Hydrogen gas, or H_2, is made up of molecules containing two hydrogen atoms each. When hydrogen is chilled to extremely low temperatures, it becomes a liquid.

Near Earth's surface, hydrogen is found only in compounds with other elements. It is one of the components of water. It is also an important part of hydrocarbons, the molecules that make up fossil fuels; carbohydrates, molecules used as food by organisms; and biomass, organic matter that can be used as fuel. Hydrogen is arguably the most important element in the universe, and it may be the most important element for the world's energy future.

Hydrogen Is an Energy Carrier

Hydrogen is not an energy source. Unlike petroleum or natural gas, it is not found in its pure state on Earth. With relatively little processing, petroleum and natural gas can be burned to release energy. Before hydrogen can be used, it must first be separated out of other chemical compounds. Hydrogen, however, is an ideal energy carrier. An energy carrier is a substance or system, such as electricity, that moves energy from one place to another. Once hydrogen is separated out of water or other compounds, it has a high energy content. The pure hydrogen can then be stored and transported to where it is needed to produce electricity.

Hydrogen's potential as an energy carrier for renewable energy sources is especially promising. Electrical energy is usually used immediately when it is produced. Renewable energy sources like wind turbines and solar panels can't produce electricity at all times. Solar panels, for example, can only generate power when the sun is out. Wind turbines stop producing electricity when the wind slows. Sometimes more energy is produced than can be used, and the excess is wasted because it is hard to store. The ability to store excess energy in an efficient way is key to the large-scale development of these **intermittent** energy technologies. Hydrogen is one solution. Excess energy produced by solar and wind power can be used to split water into

oxygen and hydrogen. The hydrogen can be stored and then used in fuel cells to produce electricity when and where it is needed. In this way, the energy originally collected by solar and wind power is stored in the hydrogen gas. Mustafa Hatipoglu, the director of a renewable energy research center, notes that as an energy carrier, hydrogen has advantages over current energy storage methods: "The energy storage capacity of batteries, even with the latest technology, is very low compared to hydrogen's storing capacity."[7]

How Is Hydrogen Produced?

As the DOE explains, "Hydrogen is abundant in our environment."[8] It is found in a wide variety of compounds on Earth. But, the DOE adds, "One of the challenges of using hydrogen as a fuel comes from being able to efficiently extract it from these compounds."[9]

Because it is so light, hydrogen accounts for only about 0.14 percent of the weight of Earth's crust. But it is found in great quantities in Earth's water and atmosphere, as well as in fossil fuels and in all plants and animals. Extracting renewable hydrogen from nonrenewable fossil fuels to produce electricity may seem like a contradictory way to address the world's energy issues. This process, however, is less polluting than burning fossil fuels for energy. The fact

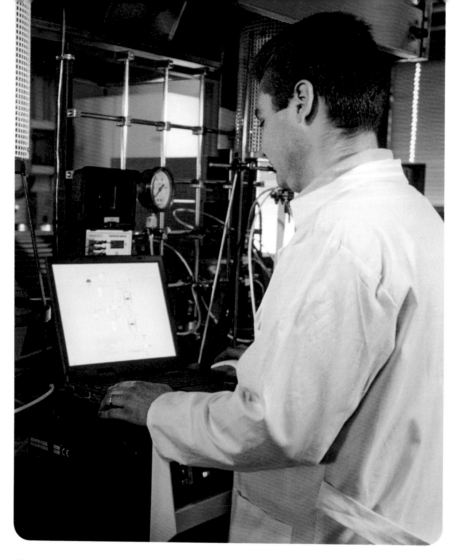

Researchers study new and better ways to produce hydrogen. This researcher is analyzing a steam-reforming reaction, a common method of hydrogen production.

that hydrogen is so abundant and found in a wide variety of sources makes it an important energy carrier. The key to a hydrogen future will be to develop the right sources and the best means to separate hydrogen from those sources. As fuel cell researcher Geoffrey Ballard explains, the critical question is, "Once you've got a fuel cell in your car, where do you get the hydrogen?"[10]

The most widely used and least expensive method for extracting pure hydrogen is steam reforming. Steam reforming uses steam under tremendous pressures and temperatures to convert natural gas or coal into hydrogen, carbon dioxide, carbon monoxide, water, and other chemicals. The hydrogen is separated out and stored. Steam reforming accounts for about 95 percent of the hydrogen used today.

Another method is gasification. It uses hot steam and oxygen to convert coal or biomass into a gaseous mixture of hydrogen, carbon monoxide, carbon dioxide, and other by-products. After further chemical reactions, the hydrogen can be separated out and purified. The DOE explains why using coal to make hydrogen can be beneficial to the United States: "The United States has an abundant, domestic resource in coal. The use of coal to produce hydrogen for the transportation sector can reduce America's total energy use and its reliance on imported petroleum while helping create jobs through the creation of a domestic industry."[11]

Hydrogen can also be produced from water using a variety of methods. One is a process called electrolysis, which uses an electric current to split water molecules into separate hydrogen and oxygen atoms. Devices that carry out electrolysis are called electrolyzers. Another way to get hydrogen from water is solar thermochemical water-splitting. This method uses high temperatures generated by solar concentrators, mirrors that focus the sun's rays into intense beams, to split water into hydrogen and oxygen. A third technique for getting hydrogen from water is a photoelectrochemical process.

In this process, hydrogen is separated out of water using sunlight and a special class of **semiconductors**. These specialized materials absorb the sunlight and use the light energy to split water molecules into hydrogen and oxygen.

Certain microbes, such as green algae and **cyanobacteria**, use sunlight to split water molecules into hydrogen and oxygen as part of their natural metabolic processes. This biological production of hydrogen is an area of great promise. Scientists are looking into altering the genes of these algae for use on a larger scale. Researcher Alex Beliaev explains the benefits of biological production: "The sustainability of our process is a solid foundation for developing an effective, renewable, and economically efficient bio-hydrogen production process."[12]

How Do Fuel Cells Work?

Fuel cell technology dates back almost 200 years. The first fuel cell was built in 1839 by the English scientist William Grove. He called it a "gas battery."[13] While Grove found his invention promising, he eventually abandoned it due to its low power output. Little work was done in the field until 1889, when a German-born British scientist, Ludwig Mond, along with his associate Charles Langer, tried replacing

Electrolysis

Electrolysis is the process of breaking something apart by passing an electric current through it. A chemical reaction takes place when an electric current passes through an electrolyte. Electrolysis can be used for many purposes. In hair removal, for example, the hair root is destroyed through electrolysis. To produce hydrogen, electrolysis breaks down water into hydrogen and oxygen. The water is made more conductive by the addition of an electrolyte, such as salt.

The chemical formula for water is H_2O. It is a compound molecule made up of two hydrogen atoms and one oxygen atom. The hydrogen atoms have a positive charge and the oxygen atom has a negative charge. During electrolysis, the water undergoes a chemical reaction that separates it into negative oxygen ions and positive hydrogen ions. The pure hydrogen ions can be separated out to be used later in a fuel cell to create electricity.

the pure hydrogen and oxygen Grove used with alternate gases. They used platinum, a type of metal, as a **catalyst**. Eventually, they abandoned their work due to the high cost of platinum.

Fifty years later, in 1939, British engineer Francis Bacon developed a fuel cell that used a heated, pressurized electrolyte. This increased the efficiency and enabled relatively inexpensive components, such as nickel, to be used instead of platinum. In 1959, Bacon demonstrated a fuel cell capable of powering a forklift

WORDS IN CONTEXT

electrolyte
A substance that conducts electricity and that can be broken up by the practice of electrolysis.

catalyst
A substance that causes a chemical reaction to happen more quickly.

Three fuel cells sit on workbenches after being removed from NASA space shuttles. Each one weighs approximately 200 pounds (91 kg).

with a capacity of 2 short tons (1.8 metric tons). Shortly thereafter, the American company Allis-Chalmers built a fuel-cell tractor.

In the 1960s, NASA developed fuels cells to power onboard equipment on spacecraft. Fuel cells that used dense liquid oxygen and liquid hydrogen provided much more electricity by weight than the best batteries available at the time. Every gram of mass is important when designing a spacecraft, so fuel cells were a natural choice for these missions. Fuel cells were also used in NASA's space shuttle program. NASA explains that its researchers continue to explore how fuel cells might be used in "systems to produce electricity and store energy on the Moon and Mars."[14]

In the mid-1970s, electric utilities in the United States, Europe, and Japan began exploring the feasibility of using fuel cells for large-scale generation of electricity. Due to numerous technical challenges associated with the immature technology, few of these studies bore immediate fruit. By the end of 2012, though, residential-scale fuel cells powered thousands of individual Japanese homes. More recently, small-scale fuel cells have been developed for powering cell phones and laptop computers.

Fuel cells resemble batteries in that they provide electricity by using chemical reactions, without the kind of mechanical devices, such as pistons or turbines, that are involved in other methods of generating power. Unlike batteries, though, fuel cells operate on a fuel that can be supplied or replenished, enabling them to continue generating power as long as they are refueled.

The most basic fuel cells generate electricity by combining hydrogen and oxygen. Normally when pure hydrogen and oxygen come into contact with one another they combine immediately to produce water vapor. The chemical reaction releases heat as a by-product. In a fuel cell, the reaction is controlled. The fuel cell contains two **electrodes**, the cathode and the anode, which are separated by an electrolyte. Hydrogen gas is introduced on one side of the cell, called the anode side. The fuel cell's catalyst strips the electrons from the hydrogen atoms, and these electrons are routed via the anode to a circuit as electrical current that can be used. The electrons travel around the circuit and back to the other side of the fuel cell, called the cathode side. Meanwhile, stripped of their electrons, the hydrogen atoms have become hydrogen ions. They travel through the electrolyte, moving from the anode to the cathode. There, they meet with the electrons coming from the circuit. Oxygen is also added here. The hydrogen ions, electrons, and oxygen combine to form water vapor, H_2O.

Variations on this basic design involve different kinds of electrolytes and various amounts of pressure and heat applied to the electrolytes. These differences are adjusted to increase efficiency, enable the cell to use fuels other than pure hydrogen, or make it possible to use cheaper materials in the electrodes.

Why Fuel Cells?

The most obvious advantage of fuel cells is their lack of harmful emissions. Fuel cells powered by hydrogen produce only pure water and heat as by-products. Even fuel cell–powered vehicles that use hydrogen produced from fossil fuels such as natural gas are estimated to "cut emissions by over 30 percent when compared with their gasoline-powered counterparts," according to the Union of Concerned Scientists.[15]

A second advantage of fuel cells is their high efficiency. Whereas conventional internal combustion engines convert less than 20 percent of the energy in their fuel into power for motion, fuel cells can use up to 60 percent of the energy stored by the hydrogen fuel.

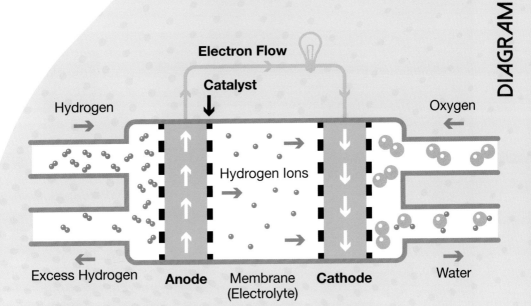

Electron Flow

Catalyst

Hydrogen

Oxygen

Hydrogen Ions

Excess Hydrogen **Anode** Membrane **Cathode** Water
(Electrolyte)

Inside a Fuel Cell

The Polymer Electrolyte Membrane (PEM) fuel cell is structured kind of like a sandwich. A membrane material in the middle is sandwiched between two electrodes, an anode and a cathode. The hydrogen enters the fuel cell at the anode side and reaches the membrane. A catalyst splits the hydrogen molecules into ions. The positively charged hydrogen ions, or protons, can pass through the electrolyte membrane. The electrons can't pass through. As the electrons start to build up, they push against each other. Eventually they push each other across the wire circuit from the anode to the cathode. The flow of electrons across the circuit is electricity, which can be used to do work, such as run a motor. The negatively charged electrons meet up on the other side with the protons and combine with oxygen from the air to make heat and water.

Simple fuel cells are built and tested in laboratories. Researchers study how to improve these devices before scaling them up for widespread use in cars.

Fuel cells also are extremely quiet, since they produce power chemically rather than mechanically.

Because of their lack of harmful emissions, their high efficiency, and their nearly silent operation, fuel cells are suited to a wide variety of applications. They can be used as power sources for service and passenger vehicles, as stationary sources of power for commercial utility grids, and as backup power sources for emergency use during utility outages. Other applications include powering individual households that lack easy access to utility grids and providing portable power sources for small items such as cell phones and laptop computers.

CAN HYDROGEN ENERGY
REPLACE FOSSIL FUELS?

The average American uses more than four times as much energy as the average person in the rest of the world. In 2014, the United States accounted for 18 percent of the total world energy consumption, despite the fact that the country had less than 5 percent of the planet's population. Clearly, the United States uses a lot of energy. Energy powers homes and businesses, moves people and goods from one place to another, and runs industries. Energy makes people's lives comfortable, convenient, and enjoyable. The rest of the world uses a lot of energy, too. This usage is expected to increase as developing nations industrialize. Providing enough energy to power the world in ways that are socially just, economically competitive, and environmentally friendly will be one of the great challenges of the coming decades.

Today, most of the energy used in the United States comes from nonrenewable energy sources such as coal, natural gas, petroleum, and uranium. Fossil fuels made up 81 percent of total energy

Fossil fuels must be pulled up from below the earth before they can be used. These pumps are extracting oil from underground wells.

consumption in 2016. The remaining 19 percent of energy used was produced by nuclear power plants (9 percent) and renewable energy, such as wind, solar, and hydropower (10 percent). Fossil fuels are energy sources that developed underground over millions of years as decaying plants and animals were exposed to heat and pressure. Different types of fossil fuels formed depending on what material was buried, for how long, and under what conditions. Coal formed from ancient plants that hardened under pressure and heat. Smaller organisms, such as zooplankton and algae, turned to oil under intense pressure. Natural gas formed similarly to oil, but the material was buried for much longer and under higher amounts of heat and pressure until it became a gas.

Because fossil fuels developed deep in the earth, they must be extracted from the ground in order to be used. There are two main ways in which people do this: mining and drilling. In mining, workers dig or scrape the ground to uncover buried coal. Surface mining can be used to expose shallow deposits of coal. Underground coal mining is needed for deeper reserves. Drilling is used to force oil and natural gas to the surface. All fossil fuels can be burned along with oxygen to provide heat. The heat can be used directly, such as in a natural gas–powered home furnaces. The heat can also be used to drive generators that produce electricity.

Extracting and burning fossil fuels significantly affects the health of the nearby environment and people. Underground coal mining is a dangerous occupation for miners. Many are injured or killed on the job each year. The Union of Concerned Scientists notes that "fatalities at underground coal mine sites in the United States totaled 77 from 2010 to 2013, including a 2010 explosion at the Upper Big Branch coal mine in West Virginia that killed 29 miners."[16] Miners also suffer from chronic health problems, such as black lung disease. Water flowing through abandoned mines can become polluted with acids and **heavy metals**. The polluted water can kill plants and animals and get into drinking water supplies. Surface mining damages ecosystems by scraping away layers of soil and even entire mountaintops. The bare soil is subject to erosion and landslides, and excess soil, rocks, and mine pollutants are dumped in local waters.

Oil and gas drilling, both onshore and offshore, brings environmental and health costs. In a process called hydraulic fracturing, or fracking, huge quantities of liquid are pumped underground to widen existing cracks in rock and release natural gas. Many of the chemicals used in the liquid can pollute local waters and are known to cause cancer and other severe health issues. The Union of Concerned Scientists explains, "One government-sponsored report found that, from 2005 to 2009, 14 oil and gas companies used 780 million gallons [2.95 billion L] of hydraulic fracturing products containing 750 chemicals and other components."[17] In addition, huge amounts of land and habitat are disturbed by wells, processing facilities, pipelines, and surrounding access roads. Some of this development occurs in wilderness areas.

Burning fossil fuels pollutes air and water all over the world. All fossil fuels emit carbon dioxide and many other harmful pollutants when burned. These pollutants include sulfur dioxide, nitrogen oxides, particulates, and mercury. Sulfur dioxide and nitrogen oxides are gases that combine with water and oxygen in the atmosphere to create sulfur and nitric acids. They then fall as **acid rain**. Acid rain damages trees and plants and

Pollution is one of the primary concerns with fossil fuels. Whether they are burned in a huge power plant or in a small car engine, they give off harmful emissions.

increases the acidity of lakes and streams, harming fish and other aquatic animals. These pollutants can also make people more likely to suffer from asthma, **bronchitis**, and other respiratory diseases.

Particulates, or soot, produce haze and can also cause bronchitis and make asthma worse. Mercury, a metal emitted from coal-fired power plants, settles on the ground and washes into lakes.

The mercury accumulates in fish and the animals that eat fish, including humans, causing neurological damage.

What Is the Greenhouse Effect?

Carbon dioxide is produced naturally by animals and humans and absorbed naturally by plants. It is also produced by the burning of fossil fuels. Carbon dioxide, methane, and a few other gases act like a giant greenhouse over Earth. They let radiation from the Sun through the atmosphere to heat Earth's surface. Some of this light normally reflects back into space. Greenhouse gases prevent it from escaping, trapping that energy in the atmosphere and heating up the planet. Some heat is good, of course. Without this greenhouse effect, people and animals would freeze to death and there would be no life on Earth. But too much of a greenhouse effect can cause the planet's temperature to rise relatively quickly. The more fossil fuels people burn, the more greenhouse gases are in the atmosphere, and the more heat is trapped.

Carbon dioxide levels in the atmosphere have been increasing steeply since the beginning of the Industrial Revolution, a period of rapid development of industry that took place in the late 1700s and early 1800s. People disagree on how much temperatures will rise and how much human-made carbon emissions are to blame. Many experts, however, believe global climate change is a crisis that will impact ecosystems, sea levels, agriculture, and human health. Former vice president Al Gore feels that advancing technology can help reduce the danger of climate change: "Electricity from the sun and the wind is now in many regions much cheaper than electricity from dirty fossil fuels. Electric cars are becoming affordable. . . . We now have a chance to use these tools to really solve the climate crisis in time to avoid the catastrophic consequences that would otherwise fall upon us."

Quoted in Terry Gross, "Al Gore Warns that Trump Is A 'Distraction' From The Issue of Climate Change," *National Public Radio,* August 2, 2017. www.npr.org.

Burning fossil fuels also releases greenhouse gases, including carbon dioxide. Greenhouse gases build up in the atmosphere over time. They trap sunlight, heating up the atmosphere. Over time this process, known as the greenhouse effect, increases the planet's average temperature. The result is known as global warming or climate change. Climate change can change weather patterns, worsening droughts and creating more powerful storms. It also melts ice near Earth's poles, raising sea levels. This can shrink islands and coastal areas or even leave them entirely underwater. For many people and governments, the environmental, health, and climate impacts of global warming are the most serious consequences of fossil fuel use.

Benefits of Hydrogen over Fossil Fuels

Fossil fuels are popular because they are relatively cheap to extract and use. People have been using fossil fuels long enough that a vast infrastructure is in place to extract, refine, deliver, and burn oil, gas, and coal. But fossil fuels are nonrenewable. It took millions of years for fossil fuels to form, and once the reserves are used, they will not be replenished. Experts and analysts disagree on the level of fossil fuel reserves remaining and how quickly we will use them. They do know that the reserves are limited and that energy use is increasing. At some point, the world will run out of fossil fuels. A handful of countries control the largest reserves of these fuels, and this can lead to economic upheaval and conflict. According to a July 2015 publication by the DOE's Fuel Cell Technologies Office, "The need for clean, domestically produced energy has never been greater."[18]

Unlike fossil fuels, the supply of hydrogen is virtually never-ending. There is more than enough water and biomass on the planet to supply hydrogen for energy. In addition, hydrogen is not concentrated in some parts of the globe; all regions of the world have hydrogen-containing resources. For the United States, using diverse, domestic resources can help keep fuel prices stable and decrease dependence on fuel imports from other countries. There is no single answer to the planet's long-term energy needs. Instead, a variety of clean energy technologies are needed to lessen dependence on fossil fuels. Hydrogen energy's strengths, including its flexibility, efficiency, and lack of pollution, may become a vital part of that portfolio of technologies.

Because hydrogen can be produced from a variety of resources, it is a flexible fuel. It can be produced in small quantities on-site for local use, including in remote places that aren't reached by power plants. Or it can be produced in large quantities at power plants and transported to its end-use site.

Hydrogen is also more efficient than fossil fuels. More of the energy in the fuel can be put to use. Hydrogen is a clean fuel, too. It produces power and heat with low or zero emissions. If hydrogen fuel is produced from fossil fuels at large centralized facilities, some emissions are created. However, producing these emissions at a central location makes it easier to monitor and reduce emissions than producing them with thousands of fossil-fuel–burning individual cars. And if the hydrogen is created using renewable resources, such as wind or solar power, the emissions are essentially zero. Cars running on hydrogen fuel cells emit only water from their tailpipes.

Hydrogen Challenges—Technical

Hydrogen has many benefits compared with fossil fuels. If it is to become a major energy carrier used widely by consumers, however, technical challenges must be addressed. Making hydrogen use practical will require advances in production, storage, and delivery.

Hydrogen exists only in compound form, and it is difficult to free from the other elements it bonds to. A lot of energy in the form of heat or electricity is needed to break those bonds. As a result, production can be costly. The greatest challenge to hydrogen production is finding ways to efficiently and economically separate hydrogen out of compounds. The amount of energy needed to split water into hydrogen and oxygen drives up production costs. Researchers are investigating ways to make electrolysis and steam reforming, the main means of hydrogen production, less expensive. The key is to be able to run the process with a minimum of energy input while still producing a lot of hydrogen. A catalyst can help. A catalyst is a substance that accelerates a chemical reaction without the need for additional energy. Researchers are looking into improved catalysts for electrolyzers.

Hydrogen production can have environmental consequences. Currently, almost all the world's hydrogen is produced from fossil fuels, either by natural gas steam reforming or coal gasification. In other words, nonrenewable resources are being used to create a clean energy carrier. Carbon dioxide, a greenhouse gas, is released

In cars, hydrogen for fuel cells must be stored at high pressure in strong tanks. Engineers must consider how to keep the tank and passengers safe in case of collisions.

in the process of separating hydrogen out of fossil fuels. Electricity generated from nonrenewable sources is often used to drive the electrolysis process that separates hydrogen out of water. When fossil fuels are used to make hydrogen, the hydrogen is not a completely clean energy source.

Storage is another challenge to widespread hydrogen energy use. Because hydrogen is such a light gas, it takes a great deal of hydrogen by volume to run a fuel cell. If stored in its natural state, huge tanks would be required. To solve this, hydrogen is stored under high pressure in specialized storage containers that can safely contain the high-pressure gas. Using high pressure to compress the hydrogen gas increases its energy density by volume, allowing for smaller containers. For small amounts of hydrogen, cylinders and stainless steel tube trailers are used. For large amounts, the best method is to store hydrogen as a dense liquid. Hydrogen turns to liquid when it is extremely cold. But the cooling process uses a great deal of energy, and the storage tanks needed for liquid hydrogen are heavy and expensive. Current research efforts are investigating materials and technologies to make hydrogen storage compact, reliable, safe, and cost-effective.

Hydrogen storage is particularly challenging when it involves FCVs. Hydrogen contains a lot of energy, but its energy by volume is much less than liquid fuels like gasoline. As a result, FCVs with a 300-mile (483-km) driving range will need storage systems that hold three to four times the volume of the gasoline tanks found in cars today. The challenge is designing FCVs that store enough hydrogen on board without sacrificing passenger and cargo space.

In addition to production and storage issues, hydrogen delivery creates some roadblocks to widespread commercialization of hydrogen energy. Once hydrogen is produced, it must be delivered to the site where it can be used, such as a refueling station or power plant. For shorter distances, hydrogen is transported by pipeline or

Is Hydrogen Safe?

For some people, the word *hydrogen* conjures images of the *Hindenburg* airship. In 1937, this massive, hydrogen-filled vessel went down in flames when attempting to land, killing thirty-six people. Because hydrogen is lighter than air, one of the earliest uses of it was as a gas to lift balloon-like airships into flight. The *Hindenburg* and its fellow airships made many successful round trips between the United States and Europe in the 1920s and 1930s before the disaster. But hydrogen is extremely flammable, meaning it burns easily when exposed to even the smallest spark.

Like the gasoline used in cars today, hydrogen is volatile and must be handled carefully. However, it has been used safely in industry for many years. Several properties make hydrogen a relatively safe gas. Hydrogen cannot catch fire in a sealed tank; oxygen is always needed for hydrogen to combust. Hydrogen's lightness means it quickly rises when released and becomes diluted into a nonflammable concentration. And finally, hydrogen does not pollute air or water when it is accidentally released. A study from the University of Miami compared the effects of a gasoline fuel tank leaking and igniting with the effects of a hydrogen fuel tank leaking and igniting. It found the FCV was much safer: "The damage to the gasoline-powered vehicle was severe. The hydrogen-powered vehicle was undamaged." Nearly the entire gasoline-powered car burst into flames. With the FCV, only a thin jet of flame came shooting out from the hydrogen tank, leaving the rest of the car intact.

Quoted in Dr. Michael R. Swain, "Fuel Leak Simulation," *US DOE*, n.d. eere.energy.gov.

over the road in pressurized tube trailers. For longer distances, hydrogen must be cooled into liquid form before transport, which is a costly procedure.

WORDS IN CONTEXT

volatile

Likely to change in a very sudden or extreme way, such as in an explosion.

Pipelines are the least expensive method for delivering large amounts of low-pressure hydrogen gas. Unfortunately, at this point the existing pipelines used for natural gas cannot be used for hydrogen. Scientists are working on ways to modify natural gas pipelines for this purpose. Approximately 1,600 miles (2,575 km) of hydrogen pipelines have been built so far, which is far less than the more than 300,000 miles (483,000 km) of natural gas pipelines crisscrossing the United States. If hydrogen is going to become a major energy source, a nationwide pipeline delivery system will need to be built, a big and costly undertaking.

Hydrogen Challenges—Economic

According to the DOE, "The greatest challenge for hydrogen production, particularly from renewable resources, is providing hydrogen at lower cost."[19] For hydrogen to compete with fossil fuels, the overall cost of hydrogen—including the cost of producing, storing, and delivering it—must be similar to the costs of fossil fuels used today. Researchers are working on new technologies that will make hydrogen production more efficient and less costly.

Hydrogen is not the only high-cost part of the equation. Fuel cells are also expensive. Progress has been made to reduce the cost. In 2016, the DOE noted that researchers had "reduced high volume automotive fuel cell costs by 50 percent since 2007."[20] Other research projects have reduced the costs of hydrogen production and delivery, reduced the cost of producing hydrogen from renewables, and broadened the commercial markets for fuel cells.

Help from the Government

Government support is vital to a hydrogen energy future. In 2009, the DOE announced funding of $41.6 million to support fuel cell technology research and development into new applications. By 2016, the department noted, the "funding [had] supported the deployment of over 1,300 fuel cell systems, exceeding the original target of 1,000."[21] Some of these projects included fuel cell forklifts for use in businesses, fuel cells for backup power in cell phone towers, and hydrogen delivery systems to remote locations. The National Renewable Energy Laboratory described the backup power fuel cells as "99.5% reliable."[22]

The State of California has been a major supporter of the FCV industry. Commercial FCV production has suffered from a chicken-and-egg problem. It's not clear what part of the infrastructure will come first—people won't buy FCVs if there are no hydrogen refueling stations, and companies won't build refueling stations if no one owns FCVs. California took steps to address this problem in 2004. Governor Arnold Schwarzenegger signed an executive order calling for the state to build a network of hydrogen fueling stations. He explained, "These stations will be used by thousands of hydrogen-powered cars and truck and buses. This starts a new era for clean California transportation. These vehicles produce no emission and no smog. They will clear the air and get rid of the smog that is hanging over our cities."[23]

A few gas stations have added hydrogen pumps alongside their traditional fuel pumps. This one is located in Washington, DC.

Progress has been made over the last several years. The DOE said that by the end of 2016, "There were 25 retail hydrogen stations open to the public, 4 retail stations in commissioning stages, and 20 more in various stages of construction or planning."[24] The California Energy Commission has authorized money through 2024 to build more hydrogen stations until there are at least 100 operational stations. California also has set a goal of having 1.5 million zero-emissions vehicles on its roads by 2035. This includes both FCVs and cars that run on electricity provided by batteries. California's efforts to build a network of fueling stations are providing researchers with practical knowledge they can use to improve FCVs and hydrogen refueling systems. According to Daniel Sperling, director of the Institute of Transportation Studies at University of California, Davis, private industry won't invest in hydrogen vehicles until there is a market for them: "The government has to be behind it. There has to be leadership."[25]

HOW DOES HYDROGEN
POWER VEHICLES?

T he use of fossil fuels for transportation is the second-largest source of carbon dioxide emissions after electric power production. Switching to cleaner transportation technologies, such as those using hydrogen fuel cells, could have a significant impact on greenhouse gas emissions.

Hydrogen has applications for vehicles at sea and in the air. Hydrogen also powers many of the rockets used to launch people and cargo into space. But the most widespread use of hydrogen in transportation has been in road vehicles. There are two types of road vehicles that use hydrogen for power: hydrogen-powered vehicles (HPV) and fuel cell vehicles (FCV). HPVs use the same basic technology as gasoline-powered engines, but they run on hydrogen fuel instead. Often, only small design adjustments are needed to adapt a basic gasoline-powered engine into a hydrogen-powered engine. However, HPVs have not become widespread.

By contrast, FCVs use hydrogen stored on board and oxygen from the air to run a fuel cell. The fuel cell produces electricity that powers an electric motor. The very first fuel cell–powered vehicle was a tractor that plowed a field in Wisconsin in October 1959. Since that first tractor, hydrogen fuel cells have powered motorcycles, buses, trains, and golf carts. But the key goal of researchers and engineers is to build a car for mass-market use. Back in the late 1990s, the world's carmakers made big promises that they would soon mass-produce cars using clean hydrogen technology. Since then, the road to progress has been slow and bumpy. But in recent years, FCV development has been gaining speed.

How Does an FCV Work?

An FCV looks and drives just like a conventional car. Instead of using a tank full of gasoline for power, however, it uses hydrogen. When hydrogen is pumped into the car at a refueling station, it travels to a carbon fiber–reinforced storage tank. The tanks are very safe and are equipped with leak detectors. In the case of an accident, hydrogen is immediately vented through a release valve on the roof of the car. The hydrogen gas is compressed at a very high pressure to increase driving range. A typical FCV tank holds between 8 to 11 pounds (4 to 5 kg) of hydrogen. By comparison, many cars have gasoline tanks that hold about 12 gallons (45 L) of fuel, which weighs around 75 pounds (34 kg).

Front intakes take in outside air and deliver it to the most important part of the FCV—the fuel cell stack. The stack combines the onboard

At a 2015 electronics trade show, Toyota showed off the inner workings of its Mirai fuel cell car. The car went on sale later that year.

hydrogen with oxygen from the outside air and turns it into electricity. When the gas pedal is depressed, the electricity from the fuel cell is sent to the electric motor. The electric motor powers the car quietly and smoothly. It is more efficient and requires less maintenance than an internal combustion engine. Like other electric cars, FCVs can use an idle-off feature, which shuts down the fuel cell at stop signs or in stopped traffic. By contrast, most internal combustion vehicles leave their engines idling during these times, wasting fuel. The FCV also has a battery that stores energy created during braking, which provides extra power to the electric motor. Like a conventional gasoline-powered car, the exhaust goes out the tailpipe. But in the case of a hydrogen fuel cell car, the only exhaust is water vapor.

Fuel Cell Vehicles on the Road

Fuel cell–powered cars have come a long way from the first fuel cell van, which was built by Daimler-Benz in 1994. This van, called NECAR, had a range of just 81 miles (130 km) before refueling. Almost the entire car was filled with the hydrogen tank and other gear, barely leaving space for the driver and a passenger. This FCV was far from perfect, but automakers didn't stop there. For the past few decades, they have been hard at work improving FCV technologies and design. By 2010, hundreds of FCVs were on the road in the United States, Europe, and Japan. Though some were restricted to use by the companies that built them, many were loaned or leased to ordinary drivers. An early entry into the FCV market was General Motors' fleet of more than one hundred fuel cell Equinox sport utility vehicles (SUVs), which hit the road in November 2007. With a full tank of hydrogen, these SUVs had a range of 200 miles (322 km).

FCV development has sped up in recent years. In early 2014, Hyundai launched the Tucson FCV, the first fuel cell car available for lease in Southern California. The carmaker pledged to produce one thousand units globally by 2015. Hyundai described the car as "one of the most futuristic vehicles on the road today."[26] That same year, Toyota announced it would have an FCV available for sale in 2016. The Toyota Mirai FCV began selling in Southern California for a price of $57,500. It has a range of more than 300 miles (480 km) on a full tank, and it takes just three to five minutes to refuel with hydrogen. Mercedes, General Motors, BMW, Nissan, and Ford have all committed to putting new FCVs on the road soon.

FCVs combine many of the benefits of internal combustion cars and battery electric cars, while eliminating some of the downsides. Internal combustion cars can be quickly refueled and can drive a long distance on a single tank of fuel. But they also produce harmful pollution. Battery electric cars are quiet and produce zero emissions when running. But they usually have shorter driving ranges, and they take hours to recharge. If the electricity they use is ultimately being produced by fossil fuels, they are still polluting.

As with many new technologies, the cost of FCVs is higher than many consumers are willing to pay. But recent improvements are making FCVs more competitive. For example, automakers have developed fuel cells that require less of the expensive metal platinum for catalysts. Very cold temperatures once caused fuel cells to freeze up, but improved fuel cells can now start quickly and drive well in these conditions. Improved storage tanks hold more pressurized hydrogen, allowing FCVs to travel for longer distances on a tank. The main roadblock to a successful consumer market for FCVs is now the lack of hydrogen-refueling stations and the supply system to deliver hydrogen to them. Hydrogen infrastructure has to compete with a worldwide network of gasoline fuel stations that has been built up over a century.

As of 2009, there were more than 200 hydrogen fueling stations in the world, though most were only for the use of the companies or institutions that operated them. California has led the way in jump-starting hydrogen infrastructure in the United States. One station developer in California explained, "We're very much at the center of this whole infrastructure thing, and I would say almost the entire thing is riding on us right now in California."[27] In Japan, eleven major

Around the World in 125 Days

Mercedes-Benz sent a convoy of three FCVs on a drive around the world in 2011, commemorating the 125th anniversary of the birth of the automobile in 1886. The three cars started at the company's headquarters in Stuttgart, Germany, and circled the globe in 125 days. The 18,750-mile (30,000-km) journey crossed four continents and fourteen countries. The first stage of the trip took the cars across France, Spain, and Portugal. From Lisbon, Portugal, the cars were flown to Miami, Florida. From there, they drove across the southern United States and then north to Vancouver in British Columbia, Canada. The cars were flown from Vancouver to Sydney, Australia. They drove across Australia to Perth, and then they were shipped by air to Shanghai and drove the rest of the way across China, Kazakhstan, Russia, and northern Europe. The FCV convoy ended back at Stuttgart. Each car could travel 250 miles (400 km) on a single full tank and needed to be refueled about 130 times. The cars were refueled by hydrogen dispensed from a support vehicle that traveled with the convoy. The FCVs performed well with no reported problems. The trip demonstrated that FCVs were ready and able to become major players on the roadways. Dieter Zetsche, the head of the company, said, "With the F-CELL World Drive we have shown that the time for electric vehicles with fuel cell has come. Now the development of the infrastructure has to pick up speed."

Quoted in "Mercedes: Fuel Cell Cars Finish World Tour, Announces H2 Stations, '14 Series Launch," *HFC Archive*, July 1, 2011. www.hfcarchive.org.

companies, including several major auto manufacturers, are working cooperatively toward building a large system of hydrogen fueling stations. The companies aim to increase FCV use by supporting hydrogen-station construction and operation and reducing costs of building and running the stations. They declared the ultimate goal for this research and development would be "the realization of a hydrogen society in Japan."[28]

In the United States, a hydrogen filling station costs about $1 million to build. According to an analysis by the University of California, Davis, the cost of building and maintaining a hydrogen infrastructure will be competitive in the marketplace once there is demand from fifty thousand to one hundred thousand vehicles. The researchers suggested that these numbers could be achieved by the end of the decade. A future direction for hydrogen fueling stations is the ability to produce hydrogen gas on demand, as the car is being filled. Just enough hydrogen would be produced to fill the car's storage tank and no more. That would eliminate the need to pressurize and store the hydrogen for future use, greatly reducing costs.

Hydrogen in Buses and Other Vehicles

Hydrogen fuel cells power a wide variety of other vehicles besides passenger cars, from buses to delivery trucks to forklifts. Buses, in fact, were one of the pioneering applications of clean-energy transportation technologies. The first fuel cell bus project in the United States started in 1987. The DOE held a competition to design and

Fuel cell buses are now in use in Switzerland. Five of the yellow buses entered use in 2011.

build a **hybrid** bus that would be used for transit at Georgetown University in Washington, DC. Multiple corporations teamed up to create the winning bus. The bus made its first trip as part of Earth Day festivities in spring 1994. Engineers continued to refine and improve the design, and by 2006 they were working on their third generation of fuel cell buses. As the program manager noted, the technology

WORDS IN CONTEXT

hybrid
Using more than one form of energy to work.

seemed ready to expand: "Part of our plan with the Generation III is to transition from the university setting to a commercial setting."[29]

Europe's first fuel cell bus, called the Eureka, was announced in 1988, though it didn't hit the road until 1994 in Brussels, Belgium. The bus was 59 feet (18 m) long and could hold eighty passengers. The fuel cell and other necessary parts of the system were housed in a two-wheeled trailer almost as long as the bus itself.

There have been many hydrogen bus projects around the world since 2000, including in the United Kingdom, the Netherlands, Brazil, and Canada. In early 2017, Aberdeen, Scotland, was running the world's largest demonstration project of hydrogen fuel cell buses. Ten public fuel cell buses, using hydrogen generated with renewable energy, served passengers around the city.

In September 2017, UPS planned to begin delivering packages in Sacramento, California, using its first electric hydrogen fuel-cell range-extended (REx) delivery trucks. The new trucks were designed in partnership with the DOE. The trucks carry a large battery pack, a hydrogen fuel cell, and stored hydrogen. The hydrogen fuel cell continuously charges the battery, which in turn powers the engine. The REx was designed to have a 125-mile (200-km) range. UPS executive Mark Wallace explained the importance of the new trucks: "This project is an essential step to test the zero tailpipe emissions technology and vehicle on the road for UPS and the transportation industry."[30]

Fuel cell–powered forklifts are at work at many companies, including FedEx, Sysco Foods, Walmart, and Coca-Cola. Forklifts are a natural fit for adaptation to fuel cell technology because they are already electric vehicles that run on batteries. Fuel cell forklifts have a few advantages over battery-powered forklifts. Batteries used in forklifts last from six to eight hours. When they run out they must be removed and recharged, and a new battery has to be installed. Batteries take eight hours to charge and eight hours to cool. Dealing with them can be a very labor- and time-intensive process. Unlike batteries, fuel cells can be refueled in a matter of minutes, much like filling a car's tank. The time spent changing and recharging batteries is saved, which boosts productivity. In addition, fuel cells can run through a whole shift without losing power, unlike battery-powered forklifts, which slow down as the battery runs down.

Hydrogen at Sea

Hydrogen fuel cells can power boats both on and under the water. In the mid-1990s, the German navy developed fuel cell–powered stealth submarines. Using a fuel cell rather than a noisy diesel engine allows the submarine to move quietly without being noticed by other vessels. One German navy captain said, "We operate in coastal waters around Europe and this submarine is specially designed for finding submarines. If you want to find other submarines of course you have to be quiet. . . . The boat is virtually undetectable."[31]

Fuel cells have found uses at sea outside of the military, too. *Zemship* is a tourism ship that travels along inland waterways. It is the first such vessel powered by fuel cells. *Zemship* began accepting passengers in the fall of 2008. The German-built ship can carry up to one hundred passengers. A year later, the Dutch *Nemo H2* fuel-cell tourist boat launched, accommodating eighty-six passengers. Fuel cell systems have also been installed and used in smaller ships, including motorboats and sailboats.

The use of hydrogen at sea goes beyond fuel cells. Some experimental boats have used hydrogen as fuel directly, just like land-based HPVs. These boats have internal combustion engines that burn hydrogen gas, generating the power to spin a propeller and move the boat forward. One example is a 33-foot (10-m) catamaran built by boat company Cheetah Marine in the United Kingdom in 2016.

The project was partly funded by the British government in an effort to demonstrate innovative new energy sources. Solar panels on the vessel's roof help run the electrolyzer that produces hydrogen. Up to 33 pounds (15 kg) of the gas are pumped into twin storage tanks on the catamaran. The hydrogen-powered engine can move the boat through the water at up to 12 knots (22 kmh). In a test run, Cheetah sent the boat on a 62-mile (100-km) voyage around the Isle of Wight, an island in the United Kingdom, a trip it completed in eight hours.

Cheetah's Lucy Strevens discussed the pioneering voyage: "We finished three hours ahead of schedule and still had enough hydrogen to circumnavigate again. It was a great success. Previously craft have been powered using hydrogen fuel cells, but it doesn't appear there's been a boat running on hydrogen in a traditional internal combustion engine."[32]

Fuel Cells in the Air

The world's first hydrogen fuel cell–powered airplane took to the air in 2008. The two-seater motor glider was converted to fuel cell power by Boeing. It went out on three test flights in February and March. On its most successful flight, it climbed to 3,300 feet (1,000 m) and flew for about twenty minutes at a relatively slow 62 miles per hour (100 kmh). A lithium-ion battery was needed to give the plane enough extra power to achieve takeoff. Despite that, the flights were a significant achievement. They demonstrated that fuel cells have a future in aerospace applications. A member of the engineering team explained, "Over the longer term, fuel-cell technology could be applied to secondary power-generating systems, such as auxiliary power units for large commercial airplanes."[33] A year and a half later, a German-built single-seater plane lifted off and flew for eight minutes on fuel cell power alone.

Short flights by small planes are a long way from big passenger planes fueled entirely by hydrogen. But researchers are looking into ways to make advances in this field. In 2011, Boeing received a patent for a ring-shaped liquid hydrogen tank that fits into a new airplane design called a blended wing body. Standard airplanes today are shaped like a long tube with wings. The blended wing body design is a triangular, tailless aircraft that merges the plane's wings and body. The tank would encircle the inside of the large cargo or passenger space of the plane, would not change the plane's aerodynamic shape, and would weigh less than conventional hydrogen tanks. Boeing has flight-tested unmanned small-scale models of the blended wing body planes in the California desert at Edwards Air Force Base. The company is working with NASA on the project.

Through a program called FUELEAP (Fostering Ultra-Efficient Low-Emitting Aviation Power), NASA researchers are also working on a new type of fuel cell that can be used to propel a big aircraft. This new fuel cell system will pull hydrogen from standard aviation gas and combine it with oxygen from the air to generate electricity. The electricity would power an all-electric or hybrid electric airplane. The fuel cell would generate energy more efficiently than in a standard airplane engine. That means that it wouldn't take as much gas to power the airplane, and the emissions would be decreased.

Though it may be challenging to use fuel cells to power large airplanes, this isn't an issue with one type of aircraft: unmanned aerial vehicles (UAVs). These remote-controlled planes are much smaller than their crewed counterparts. They often carry powerful cameras and sensors that let them carry out surveillance missions. UAVs are best known through their military use, but firefighters, telecommunications workers, and pipeline inspectors can also take advantage of aerial surveillance. Small-scale aircraft powered by hydrogen fuel cells may represent a way to accomplish these missions with less use of fossil fuels.

Hydrogen Fuels Space Exploration

NASA has used fuel cells aboard its spacecraft since the 1960s to generate electricity for the vehicles' systems. The by-product was pure water, which the crew could then drink. Hydrogen has another use in the space program—it is also used as a propellant for launching rockets into space. Figuring out how to use liquid hydrogen as a rocket propellant was one of NASA's most significant technical achievements.

Hydrogen is a perfect rocket fuel. It burns quickly and with extreme intensity at 5,500°F (3,040°C). When it combines with liquid oxygen, liquid hydrogen creates the highest specific impulse of any known rocket propellant.

On the space shuttles, liquid hydrogen was stored in a large orange tank attached to the shuttle. The three engines at the shuttle's base burned this hydrogen along with oxygen to propel the spacecraft.

Specific impulse is the efficiency of a fuel in relation to the weight of the fuel used. The less fuel needed to propel a particular rocket, the higher the specific impulse.

Hydrogen, however, has properties that made adapting it for use as a rocket fuel technically challenging. Overcoming those challenges took a tremendous amount of technical innovation. Hydrogen can only be turned into a liquid at an extremely low temperature. To maintain it in liquid form, hydrogen must be stored at −423°F (−253°C). It must then be handled carefully so that it doesn't heat up. Rockets fueled with liquid hydrogen must be very well insulated from all sources of heat. On takeoff, rocket engine exhaust and the **friction** during flight through Earth's atmosphere create heat. Once the rocket is in space, the hydrogen tank must be insulated from the heat of the Sun. If the hydrogen heats up, it will evaporate or boil off. As it heats up, hydrogen expands rapidly, so the tank must be vented to keep it from exploding. Tanks must be constructed extremely carefully. When metals are exposed to the extreme cold of liquid hydrogen, they become brittle. In addition, the tiny hydrogen atoms can leak through the tiniest pores and cracks in welded seams.

> ## WORDS IN CONTEXT
>
> ### friction
> The force of resistance to motion when objects or surfaces move against each other.

Finding a way to detect hydrogen leaks quickly and easily became a top priority for rocket engineers because hydrogen is flammable when it hits the air. Detecting leaks is made more difficult by the fact that hydrogen gas has no color or odor. In the Apollo space program days of the late 1960s and early 1970s, leaks were detected using what NASA workers called the "broom test."[34] Workers walked around the rocket with a broom head stretched out in front of them. If the broom head began to burn, they knew there was a leak.

Researchers developed news ways to detect leaks, but these methods had drawbacks. Sensors installed in a permanent place may not be able to monitor every part of a rocket. Handheld sensors require technicians to walk slowly around the vehicle, listening for a beeping sound. When a technician hears a beep, it can be difficult to tell exactly what spot on the vehicle caused the sensor to beep. A new technology developed by the Kennedy Space Center and the University of Central Florida allows technicians to see hydrogen leaks. The technology is a special tape that changes color through a chemical reaction when it is exposed to hydrogen. It detects a leak quickly, and technicians can see exactly where the leak is. NASA researcher Luke Roberson explained that the tape was used alongside other methods when searching for a particular hydrogen leak in the space shuttle launch equipment in 2007: "Sensors were successful in identifying that there was a leak. The tape helped pinpoint the exact location."[35] The tape is now used in oil and gas production, power generation, and chemical production industries to enhance safety.

4

IS THE HYDROGEN ECONOMY IN OUR FUTURE?

Hydrogen energy and fuel cell technologies continue to evolve and improve. As a result, more businesses and industries are using hydrogen energy to help fill their electricity needs. They are also investigating more ways to bring hydrogen-based fuel cells to the consumer market. Cost, however, remains a significant barrier to more widespread use of hydrogen energy. Researchers are currently exploring new ways to produce, store, and deliver hydrogen that will not only reduce its cost, but also improve and expand the infrastructure to get hydrogen to new users. In addition to transportation, emerging markets for hydrogen include power plants for large-scale energy production and smaller fuel cell systems that can power individual homes. In the future, hydrogen may even be used as a clean energy source to power nuclear reactors. It will also continue to play a role in the rockets that enable us to explore the solar system.

Artificial Photosynthesis

In the field of hydrogen production, research is aimed at lowering both initial capital costs and ongoing operating costs. On the capital side, progress is being made in the development of low-cost alternatives to expensive catalyst materials such as platinum. A company called HyperSolar, for example, has developed a device that mimics the natural process of photosynthesis. In nature, this process allows plants to break water down into hydrogen and oxygen, so they can be combined with carbon in order to create food for the plant. In HyperSolar's device, water is split into hydrogen and oxygen without the need for the usual expensive platinum catalyst. The company explained that tests have been very promising: "Test results indicate that this low cost catalyst will . . . improve hydrogen production efficiency, and further reduce the cost of the Company's hydrogen production process."[36]

This is only one of several ongoing projects to develop a sort of artificial leaf capable of using the sun's power to divide water into its component elements. Other research in artificial photosynthesis is ongoing at the California Institute of Technology; the University of California, Santa Barbara; the University of Tokyo in Japan; and other locations. Overall, artificial photosynthesis remains a major challenge. John Turner of the US National Renewable Energy Laboratory explains that decades of research have revealed the task to be even tougher than scientists expected: "This is a really, really difficult, challenging problem. The payback would be huge, but it's not as simple as everyone wanted it to be when we started playing in this area 40 years ago."[37]

Storage and Delivery

In the field of hydrogen storage and delivery, current research is aimed at improving energy density while lowering costs. While hydrogen contains more energy by *mass* than most other fuels, it is extremely light. This means it has much lower energy density by *volume* than liquid fuels such as gasoline. As a result, in order for sufficient quantities to be stored, hydrogen must be compressed or otherwise condensed. This has commonly been accomplished using special vessels to store gaseous hydrogen at high pressure. These containers consist of a plastic liner strengthened with a wrap of expensive carbon-fiber composite material. Efforts are underway to develop alternative materials and manufacturing processes that can lower the cost of hydrogen storage containers. Longer-term solutions being explored include low-temperature, or cryogenic, storage, which can allow liquid hydrogen to be stored at higher energy densities while lowering storage pressures. For low-temperature or cryogenic storage to be feasible, insulated storage systems must be improved to prevent heat from entering vessels. Further research involves technologies to store hydrogen at high densities and low pressures by binding it into compounds or **adsorbing** it onto the surfaces of solids. The key difficulty in these technologies

WORDS IN CONTEXT

adsorbing
The process in which a gas, liquid, or solid adheres to the surface of a solid but does not penetrate it.

Researchers study ways to store hydrogen safely using solid materials. This scientist is performing a study at Brookhaven National Laboratory in New York.

is to ensure they are cost-effective, able to store hydrogen at a high density, and able to quickly take in and give off the hydrogen they store.

Methods for transporting hydrogen include pipelines carrying low-pressure gaseous hydrogen, tube trailers carrying high-pressure gaseous hydrogen, and tankers carrying cryogenic liquid hydrogen. Pipelines are a relatively inexpensive delivery method for low pressure gas, though they do require a large initial capital investment for construction. Researchers are investigating options for lower-cost pipelines. One possibility is to use fiber-reinforced polymer (FRP) pipelines, which would cost about 20 percent less to install than conventional steel pipelines. FRP pipelines also may be more reliable for hydrogen delivery than steel, because hydrogen can cause steel to become brittle. Possible interactions between hydrogen and steel, as well as other possible pipe materials, need to be explored as part of the quest for savings in pipeline construction. Another research direction is examining ways to adapt existing natural gas pipelines to accommodate either a mix of natural gas and hydrogen or pure hydrogen.

Pressurized tube trailers are used to move smaller amounts of hydrogen 200 miles (320 km) or less. For longer distances, if there are no pipelines available, liquefied hydrogen, which has been cooled to −423°F (−253°C), is hauled in cryogenic tank trucks. The process of liquefying hydrogen is energy intensive, though, requiring more than 30 percent of the energy content of the hydrogen. This makes liquid hydrogen a relatively costly option.

Fuel Cell Power Plants

Electric utility companies began investigating how hydrogen fuel cells could be used in power plants as far back as the 1960s. Steep costs and technical difficulties have led to highs and lows in these efforts. Typically, when oil prices are high, there is more incentive to develop alternative energy sources. When oil prices drop, so do the incentives. With the recent emphasis on reducing carbon dioxide emissions worldwide, hydrogen fuel cell power plant projects are back in action.

A solar-to-hydrogen power plant has provided electricity for the French island of Corsica in the Mediterranean Sea since December 2011. The 0.56-megawatt (MW) solar power plant uses a combination of solar energy devices, electrolyzers, hydrogen storage, and fuel cells. During the day when the sun is out, electricity is produced with solar energy. The solar energy powers electrolyzers to produce hydrogen, which is stored. The hydrogen powers fuel cells during the night to produce electricity. A similar wind-to-hydrogen power plant opened in Prenzlau, Germany, the same year. The 6-MW plant is primarily a wind power plant, but in periods of excess energy, it uses electricity from the wind turbines to generate hydrogen by electrolysis. The stored energy in the hydrogen powers fuel cells when little or no wind is available. The plant also provides hydrogen to refueling stations in Berlin and Hamburg.

The Fountain Valley tri-generation power plant began operation in California in 2014. The same year, the world's largest fuel cell plant opened in South Korea. The fuel cells run on natural gas converted to hydrogen. The plant provides electricity to heat and power homes in the city of Hwaseong. The facility is the first of several fuel cell projects planned in the Seoul area. A 20-MW fuel cell park opened in Seoul in early 2017 and took only ten months to build. The Seoul power plant uses technologies from a US-based company.

Currently, fuel cell power plants are not able to compete with large and relatively inexpensive fossil fuel–fired power plants in most markets. Each new fuel cell power plant, however, improves the technology and cost-effectiveness of these systems. The new plants demonstrate that hydrogen fuel cells can deliver large amounts of clean electricity to power grids.

Backed Up by Hydrogen

One emerging market for hydrogen fuel cells consists of businesses and industries that require steady backup power during power outages. Backup power (BUP) systems allow key services, such as telecommunications and hospitals, to keep functioning during storms and other times when steady power is not available from the main power grid. During Hurricane Sandy, which struck the East Coast

Critical pieces of infrastructure, such as cell phone towers, can have their power sources damaged or disabled by storms or other natural disasters. Backup systems, including ones powered by hydrogen fuel cells, can help keep these things running during such emergencies.

in 2012, cell phone towers that had BUP systems powered by fuel cells continued working with no problems. The need for reliable emergency power is increasing in the United States. The DOE noted in a 2012 report that, "The number of grid outages in the United States has increased over the last decade . . . with an average outage of approximately 42 hours between 2002 and 2012."[38] Grid outages will continue to increase if global warming leads to more frequent extreme weather, which is predicted by many climate scientists.

Fuel cell BUP systems are more reliable and require less maintenance than conventional diesel generators that are used for backup power, and they typically can run for more than sixty-five hours. In addition, they are quieter, have lower or no harmful emissions, and can be monitored remotely, making them an excellent backup power source, particularly in remote areas.

Hydrogen-Powered Homes and Businesses

The Institute of Gas Technology exhibited a futuristic "Home for Tomorrow" in the 1960s. The Institute said the home was powered by "reformed natural gas," which it called a "new super active form of natural gas."[39] In fact, this gas was mostly hydrogen. Though the model home was never built for commercial use, it gave scientists and researchers insight into the benefits and technical challenges of using hydrogen in homes.

Fuel cells are a promising source of electricity for homes and businesses for several reasons. When electricity and heat are both produced from a single source of fuel, it is called combined heat and power (CHP). When done on the scale of a single house, such as with natural gas, it is called micro-CHP. Fuel cells work well for micro-CHP because they produce both heat and electricity. In addition, fuel cells are more efficient than conventional electricity generation methods. So even when fossil fuels are used in generating the hydrogen, carbon dioxide emissions are significantly reduced.

Despite the promise of hydrogen, there are relatively few homes and businesses that run entirely on fuel cells. A few experimental hydrogen-powered homes were built in the 1980s, including one in Sweden and one in California. Also in California, the Sierra Nevada

Brewery in Chico uses natural gas and methane to produce hydrogen for fuel cells. Its fuel cells produce enough electricity to power the entire production plant. Ken Grossman, the company's CEO, explained the thought process behind using fuel cells:

> While our brewery requires reliable power 24/7, Sierra Nevada also is committed to energy efficiency and reducing our environmental impact on the Chico community. We decided to buy and install a 1-MW Direct FuelCell power plant for two main reasons: its far lower emissions than those of a conventional power plant and its ability to produce the high-value heat by-product our brewing process requires. [This] was the most cost-effective and environmentally favorable on-site power generation solution for us.[40]

Currently there are several national residential fuel cell programs in Europe and Korea. Japan, however, leads the way in this area. In the 1990s, the Japanese government began Ene-Farm, a fuel cell project to heat and power private homes. Fuel cells able to produce enough energy for a home were developed. The systems are available from regional gas companies, which also provide the hydrogen gas. The Japanese government helps with the cost of installing the fuel cells in private homes. By 2012, more than twenty thousand fuel cell systems to heat and power homes in Japan were operating, with more expected soon. Kentaro Horisaka, the general manager of a fuel cell planning group, spoke about the benefits of these systems:

The concept is that you can lead your normal, comfortable life,

you get plenty of power, you get plenty of hot water, but you're

still saving energy, you're still helping . . . society save [carbon

dioxide]. . . . In comparison to owning a normal electric and

gas system this ENE-FARM will save 1.3 tonnes [1.4 short tons]

of [carbon dioxide] each year.[41]

The Hydrogen House

Mike Strizki completed his new home in 2006—North America's first solar-hydrogen powered home. Strizki built the house near Hopewell, New Jersey, with help from a grant from the New Jersey Board of Public Utilities. Solar panels throughout the property collect energy from the Sun. The solar energy is collected in a battery, which runs an electrolyzer to split water into hydrogen and oxygen. The hydrogen is stored in low-pressure propane tanks, similar to ones used at gas stations. Strizki burns the pure hydrogen for cooking and uses it to heat the house in place of a conventional natural gas furnace. He also uses the hydrogen to power fuel cells that provide electricity for the house, as well as his fuel cell car.

The house also has a geothermal heat system. The geothermal, solar, and hydrogen systems combined provide all the power needed for his home and car, which means that Strizki pays no utility bills. What's more, he actually sells the extra electricity produced by his systems back to the utility company for as much as $20,000 a year. Strizki says, "No one knows where the fuel prices are going to go. This is hedging your bet—that you are your own power plant, and that you're independent of the grid. So you're not vulnerable."

"The Hydrogen House," *Hydrogen House*, n.d. www.hydrogenhouseproject.org.

Hydrogen Fusion

Nuclear power is a source of energy that does not require the use of fossil fuels. In nuclear power plants, the radioactive elements uranium and plutonium undergo fission. In this process, atoms of these elements are split apart, releasing energy. The same basic reaction takes place inside nuclear weapons, causing huge explosions. In power plants, the fission process is carefully controlled to release energy safely as heat. The heat boils water into steam, which then spins a turbine to generate electricity.

One advantage of nuclear power is that it can generate a great deal of energy without producing greenhouse gases. Like fossil fuels, however, uranium and plutonium are nonrenewable resources. Their radioactivity also makes them dangerous. Nuclear power plants create waste that remains radioactive and hazardous for thousands of years. It must be transported to sites where it can be carefully stored. If there is an accident at a nuclear power plant, radioactive material can be released into the environment, harming plants and animals.

Whereas the fission process splits atoms apart, the fusion process joins atoms together. This is the basic process that hydrogen undergoes in the Sun. It releases enormous amounts of energy. Future nuclear power plants may use fusion instead of fission. A fusion plant could use ordinary water, rather than radioactive elements, as fuel. It would produce no harmful wastes.

However, researchers have a great deal of work to do before such power plants can be built. Hydrogen fusion requires extremely high temperatures. The Sun is hot enough to sustain constant nuclear fusion, but such conditions are hard to achieve on Earth. A nuclear fusion plant will require temperatures of 100 million°F (56 million°C) or more to work. Unfortunately, the technology needed to economically and safely create a hydrogen fusion reaction in a commercial setting may be decades away. Still, today's researchers are laying the groundwork for a hydrogen-fueled future made possible by fusion.

This research can cost a lot of money, but many scientists believe it is worth the expense. Researcher Thomas Pedersen says, "If you look at it in terms of energy budgets, or what's spent on military development, it's not really a lot of money that's going to this. If you compare us to other research projects, it seems very expensive, but if you compare it to what goes into oil production or windmills or subsidies for renewables, it's much, much less than that."[42]

Deep Space Exploration

NASA is continuing to make progress toward the goal of sending humans deeper into the solar system than ever before. The agency hopes to send astronauts to Mars in the next few decades. Those astronauts may ride on the Space Launch System (SLS). This enormous rocket is fueled by liquid hydrogen and liquid oxygen. NASA notes that it will be "the world's most powerful rocket" once it is fully developed.[43] SLS will be able to carry large payloads to asteroids, the moon, and Mars.

Reaching these far-flung destinations is only the first step. In order to survive for any length of time on other planets, astronauts will need to live off the land, just as explorers and settlers on Earth developed ways to use the local resources. The *Lunar Prospector* mission, launched in 1998, sent a probe to the moon to explore its resources. *Lunar Prospector* detected large amounts of hydrogen in both of the moon's polar regions—likely in the form of water. More recent explorations in 2008 and 2009 again located potential water on the moon. If there is water, there is both hydrogen and oxygen on the moon. This means astronauts could stop there for refueling. Astronauts could fill up with fresh water to drink. Splitting the water into hydrogen and oxygen would provide rocket propellant and breathable air. The elements could be used as a power source, too. Jack Fox of NASA says, "By separating these elements, we have what it takes to operate fuel cells to create electricity. That gives us a power plant on a distant destination."[44]

The Future of Hydrogen Energy

Research is ongoing in the production, storage, and delivery of hydrogen. This work has the potential to move society toward a hydrogen economy. Whether or not that happens depends on progress being made in a number of areas. In general, advances need to be made in cost reduction, efficiency, and durability.

Hydrogen has the potential to provide the world with a virtually unlimited source of energy that would greatly reduce reliance on fossil fuels, reduce air pollution, and limit the release of greenhouse gases into the atmosphere. The world has been making slow progress toward the hydrogen economy first dreamed of in the 1970s.

The last few decades have seen an increase in the development of hydrogen-based technologies and applications for clean energy. But widespread use of hydrogen energy is not yet a reality.

The first serious steps toward a hydrogen economy were taken in the 1990s. At the end of that decade, Iceland announced its goal to become the first hydrogen-based economy within thirty to forty years. Other countries followed with plans to supply some or all of their energy from renewable sources, including hydrogen. In the early 2000s, Hawaii and Vanuatu, a small island in the South Pacific, began expanding their hydrogen use. In 2004, California, the largest consumer of gasoline in the United States, began developing the world's first "hydrogen highway," a system of hydrogen production plants and refueling stations to support a fleet of hydrogen fuel cell cars on its roads.

There are, of course, other resources and technologies in the race to replace fossil fuels, including solar, wind, and hydropower. Each will likely play a role in a diverse portfolio of renewable energy sources. The case for hydrogen and fuel cells as a significant part of that portfolio was made in a 2008 report by the National Research Council. The report predicted that "the deepest cuts in oil use and [carbon dioxide] emissions after about 2040 would come from hydrogen."[45] As the world's thirst for energy grows, along with the environmental costs of energy production and use, hydrogen may provide the world with an opportunity to create a clean energy future.

INTRODUCTION: NATURE'S FUEL

1. Quoted in Susan Carpenter, "Fountain Valley Hydrogen Station Fills 'er Up with Sewer Gas," *Los Angeles Times*, August 11, 2011. latimesblogs.latimes.com.

2. Quoted in Julia Pyper, "Sewage Could Provide Fuel of the Future," *Scientific American*, November 19, 2014. www.scientificamerican.com.

3. Quoted in Bob Granath, "Liquid Hydrogen—the Fuel of Choice for Space Exploration," *NASA*, October 20, 2015. www.nasa.gov.

4. Quoted in Tina Casey, "One Step Closer to the Hydrogen Economy Dream," *Clean Technica*, June 30, 2016. www.cleantechnica.com.

5. Quoted in Julia Pyper, "Will the Most Common Molecule in the Universe Be the Fuel of the Future?" *E&E News*, November 18, 2014. www.eenews.net.

CHAPTER 1: HOW DOES HYDROGEN ENERGY WORK?

6. Quoted in Neil deGrasse Tyson, "The Periodic Table of the Cosmos," *Natural History*, July 1, 2002. www.haydenplanetarium.org.

7. Quoted in Julia Harte, "GP Exclusive Interview: Turkey Beginning to Lay Infrastructure for Hydrogen Economy," *Green Prophet*, July 1, 2011. www.greenprophet.com.

8. Quoted in "Hydrogen Basics," *US Department of Energy*, n.d. afdc. www.energy.gov.

9. Quoted in "Hydrogen Basics."

10. Quoted in Tariq Malik, "Fuel Cell Pioneer: An Interview with Geoffrey Ballard," *Scientific American*, n.d. www.scientificamerican.com.

11. Quoted in "Hydrogen Production: Coal Gasification," *US Department of Energy*, n.d. www.energy.gov.

12. Quoted in "Sustained Hydrogen Production from Cyanobacteria in the Presence of Oxygen," *Science X*, October 12, 2012. www.phys.org.

13. Quoted in "Fuel Cell Origins: 1840-1890," *Smithsonian Institute of American History*, n.d. americanhistory.si.edu.

14. Quoted in Justin Fitzgerald and Nancy O'Bryan, "Fuel Cells: A Better Source for Earth and Space," *NASA*, February 11, 2005. www.nasa.gov.

15. Quoted in "How Do Hydrogen Fuel Cell Vehicles Work?" *Union of Concerned Scientists*, n.d. www.ucsusa.org.

CHAPTER 2: CAN HYDROGEN ENERGY REPLACE FOSSIL FUELS?

16. Quoted in "The Hidden Costs of Fossil Fuels," *Union of Concerned Scientists*, n.d. www.ucsusa.org.

17. Quoted in "The Hidden Costs of Fossil Fuels."

18. Quoted in "Clean, Efficient, and Reliable Power for the 21st Century," *US Department of Energy*, July 2015. www.energy.gov.

19. Quoted in "Hydrogen Production," *US Department of Energy*, April 2016. www.energy.gov.

20. Quoted in "Progress and Accomplishments in Hydrogen and Fuel Cells," *US Department of Energy*, April 2016. www.energy.gov.

21. Quoted in "Highlights from U.S. Department of Energy's Fuel Cell Recovery Act Projects," *US Department of Energy*, April 2016. www.energy.gov.

22. Quoted in "Highlights from U.S. Department of Energy's Fuel Cell Recovery Act Projects."

23. Quoted in Deborah Ziff, "Hydrogen Hopes," *Mother Jones*, May 4, 2004. www.motherjones.com.

24. Quoted in "Hydrogen Basics."

25. Quoted in Jeff Wise, "The Truth About Hydrogen." *Popular Mechanics,* November 31, 2006. www.popularmechanics.com.

CHAPTER 3: HOW DOES HYDROGEN POWER VEHICLES?

26. Quoted in "Tucson Fuel Cell," *Hyundai USA*, n.d. www.hyundaiusa.com.

27. Quoted in Julian Pyper, "Will the Most Common Molecule in the Universe be the Fuel of the Future?"

28. Quoted in James Ayre, "Large-Scale Buildout of Hydrogen Vehicle Refueling Stations Backed by 11 Major Japanese Companies," *Clean Technica*, May 26, 2017. www.cleantechnica.com.

29. Quoted in Kate Mays, "University Developing New Fuel Cell Bus," *Georgetown Voice*, October 5, 2006. www.georgetownvoice.com.

30. Quoted in James Ayre, "UPS to Deploy 1st Electric Hydrogen REx Trucks in September," *Clean Technica*, May 5, 2017. www.cleantechnica.com.

31. Quoted in Frederik Pleitgen, "Super-Stealth Sub Powered by Fuel Cell," *CNN*, February 22, 2011. www.cnn.com.

32. Quoted in "World's First Hydrogen Powered Boat Smashes Targets," *Cheetah Marine*, May 11, 2016. www.cheetahmarine.co.uk.

33. Quoted in Tom Koehler, "A Green Machine," *Boeing Frontiers*, May 2008. www.boeing.com.

34. Quoted in "Invisible Flame Imaging," *NASA*, n.d. spinoff.nasa.gov.

35. Quoted in Bob Granath, "Innovative Hydrogen Leak Detection Tape Earns Prestigious Award," *NASA*, October 20, 2015. www.nasa.gov.

CHAPTER 4: IS THE HYDROGEN ECONOMY IN OUR FUTURE?

36. Quoted in Tina Casey, "Solar Energy Fuels HyperSolar's Hydrogen Dream," *Clean Technica*, January 29, 2016. www.cleantechnica.com.

37. Quoted in Jessica Marshall, "Solar Energy: Springtime for the Artificial Leaf," *Nature*, June 4, 2014. www.nature.com.

38. Quoted in "Early Markets: Fuel Cells for Backup Power," *US Department of Energy*, October 2014. www.energy.gov.

39. Quoted in Peter Hoffman. *Tomorrow's Energy*. Cambridge, MA: MIT P, 2012. p. 236.

40. Quoted in Dr. Robert Peltier, "1-MW Fuel Cell Cogeneration Project, Sierra Nevada Brewing Co., Chico, California," *Power*, August 15, 2006. www.powermag.com.

41. Quoted in Anmar Frangoul, "In Japan, Natural Gas and Innovation Are Changing the Way Homes Are Powered," *CNBC*, May 18, 2017. www.cnbc.com.

42. Quoted in Nathaniel Scharping, "Why Nuclear Fusion Is Always 30 Years Away," *Discover*, March 23, 2016. blogs.discovermagazine.com.

43. Quoted in Jennifer Harbaugh, "Preparing to Plug Into NASA SLS Fuel Tank," *NASA*, December 21, 2016. www.nasa.gov.

44. Quoted in Bob Granath, "NASA's Exploration Plans Include Living Off the Land," *NASA*, June 1, 2015. www.nasa.gov.

45. Peter Hoffman. *Tomorrow's Energy*. Cambridge, MA: MIT P, 2012. p. 292.

BOOKS

Lester R. Brown with Janet Larsen, J. Matthew Roney, and Emily E. Adams, Earth Policy Institute, *The Great Transition: Shifting from Fossil Fuels to Solar and Wind Energy.* New York: W. W. Norton & Company, 2015.

Bridget Heos, *It's Getting Hot in Here: The Past, the Present, and the Future of Climate Change.* Boston: Houghton Mifflin Harcourt, 2015.

Peter Hoffmann, *Tomorrow's Energy: Hydrogen, Fuel Cells, and the Prospects for a Cleaner Planet.* Cambridge, MA: MIT Press, 2012.

Geoffrey B. Holland and James J. Provenzano, *The Hydrogen Age: Empowering a Clean-Energy Future.* Salt Lake City, UT: Gibbs Smith, 2007.

Jeremy Shere, *Renewable: The World-Changing Power of Alternative Energy.* New York: St. Martin's Press, 2013.

WEBSITES

Clean Technica
http://cleantechnica.com

The website collects and publishes news stories, reviews, and commentary focusing on clean transport, renewable power sources, and energy efficiency.

Department of Energy: Fuel Cell Technologies Office
https://energy.gov/eere/fuelcells/fuel-cell-technologies-office

The website of the Department of Energy's Fuel Cell Technologies Office focuses on research, development, and innovation to advance the use of hydrogen and fuel cells.

Department of Energy: Office of Energy Efficiency & Renewable Energy
https://www.energy.gov/eere/office-energy-efficiency-renewable-energy

This website from the Department of Energy focuses on clean, affordable, and efficient energy sources, including hydrogen and fuel cells for transportation.

Fuel Cell Today
http://fuelcelltoday.com

This website covers trends, news, policies, and developments in the fuel cell industry.

US Energy Information Administration
http://www.eia.gov

Learn about the United States' production and consumption of all energy sources, including fossil fuels, nuclear, and renewable, at the website for the USEIA.

ABOUT THE AUTHOR

Yvette LaPierre lives in Grand Forks, North Dakota, with her husband, two daughters, two dogs, and two crested geckos. She hopes her next car will be a hydrogen FCV.